WILLING TO BE SET FREE

Kingdom Principles for Living Victoriously

John 6:40 — *"And this is the will of Him who sent Me, that everyone who sees the Son and believes in Him may have everlasting life…"*

Book 2

Nancy Williams

Way of Life Publishing

DEDICATION

To those who read this:

> This is dedicated to you, in the hopes that through this book you will find a deeper meaning in your walk with Christ. I hope a living Christianity will be yours. That you feel how much you are loved; that you see more clearly how the Bible applies to you and that you will then embrace and incorporate these principles into your way of being and living.

I want to thank and acknowledge my loving husband, Jaycee, and daughter, Natalie, for lovingly and graciously supporting me as I took time away to complete this labor of love.

PREMISE FOR THIS WORK

Based on Romans 3:23, where God says that all have sinned and fall short of the glory of God, it is this book's premise that all of us require healing. We believe it is through sin, starting with Adam and Eve and passed down from generation to generation, that dysfunctional patterns began. It is sin that separates us from God, says Isaiah 59:2.

It is our goal to facilitate:

> 1st — Looking at ourselves honestly
>
> 2nd—Accepting God's grace, love, and truth so that
>
> 3rd —We can be set free from our sins

We propose to do this by using God's Word and following His way.

We believe the fruit of this will be:

- An intimate relationship with God the Father, God the Son, and God the Holy Spirit

- The abundant life from God will be ours as we live and grow in this dynamic relationship

- Manifestation of the gifts of the Spirit in us which is for the profit of all and that God gives as He sees fit and when He sees fit (1 Corinthians 12:7-11). These gifts of the spirit include:

  a. Word of wisdom

  b. Word of knowledge

c. Faith

d. Gift of healing

e. Working of miracles

f. Gift of prophecy

g. Discerning of spirits

h. Gift of tongues

i. Interpretation of tongues

HOW TO USE THESE CHAPTERS

Bringing sinful patterns to the surface and dealing with them according to God's principles will restore your path in life and repair the breach separating you from others and from God, as stated in Isaiah 58:12. Individuals who have gone through this book have found the Holy Spirit and stated that they were empowered and enabled to trust God and look honestly at their lives.

God calls you and all of us to live a principled life. As you incorporate His principles in this book, the Holy Spirit will naturally flow through you to others. This book will cover 3 of God's principles and a growth plan that emphasizes God's principles, as found in the Bible, as the only source of living victoriously. As God created the world and set up universal principles by which it operates, relational principles are found within this creation and the Bible. He and His principles are the source of life and as you incorporate them, your life will flow smoothly with less turmoil and more success. Therefore, memorize the given scriptures and the Holy Spirit will bring them to your remembrance in your time of need. "God's Word will not return void" (Isaiah 55:11). You will be affected by memorizing His Word even if you do not feel that an impact is being made. In each chapter, answer the questions to the best of your ability and you will be amazed at what starts happening within you!

This work is divided into 4 books which can be completed separately or sequentially by yourself or within a group setting.

If going through A Way of Life in a group setting, the facilitator may decide to share a short weekly teaching that provides the biblical foundation for the principle/s being reviewed, such as confession or repentance. The main group could then be divided into groups with a group facilitator present to promote sharing what God is doing in each other's lives, what the chapter review has brought to light, and any hindrance in depending on God. The main facilitator may bring the whole group back together at the end for sharing and prayer or each group could end their time with prayer.

Additional supportive subjects are found in the appendix at the back of each book in this series of 4.

And now, let us continue with discovering and applying God's Kingdom Principles for Living Victoriously!

INTRODUCTION

Book 2 will explore what has happened in your life, your family of origin, and how you emotionally handled these events. Learning to bring these events to light will remove the power they have over you, your life, and your behaviors. In Book 2, you will learn how to safely talk to one another so that you can be healed and any power of sin can be broken over you. I am excited for you! Stay the course. It's not always easy but it's worth it.

Let's start this book by looking at your identity as a child of the Most High God. ☺

You are created in the image of God and hence, are very valuable and precious in His sight and loved unconditionally. You also have a purpose that you were born to fulfill and as you draw close to God and His way, you will become aware of and can then live out what was ordained for you from the beginning of time.

The Westminster Catechism states, in question 1 with the answer:

- "Q. 1. What is the chief end of man?
- Man's chief end is to glorify God and to enjoy him forever. 1 Cor. 10:31; Rom. 11:36; Ps. 73:25-28."

So, your goal is to get to know God and enjoy Him and as you do that (and in spite of), He enjoys you as well!

Before beginning, it's important to evaluate how you show up in life and look at how Jesus showed up, as He is our example to follow. You might be wondering, "What is meant by how you show up?" In relationships with others, this means, are your moods and spirit happy, anxious, sad, overbearing, funny, serious, demanding, irritating, or goofy, to name a few. It's what you dole or give out to others and their experience of you. Jesus showed up with tough yet unconditional love for others and knew their heart motives and feelings. The way He showed up was compassionate and He listened well. Jesus could tell when the religious leaders were trying to trick Him and called them out about it. His heart was one for them to understand the will of His Father and for them to hear Him, but the religious rulers did not. Those that did, allowed Him to change them from the inside out as they got revelation or understanding about what love truly is and how God calls us to act, or *be, from the inside out.*

WHAT DOES IT MEAN TO BE?

You might have heard well-meaning messages about loving one another and treating each other with compassion and kindness while doing what's right. And yet, this message misses the mark. You might attempt to *put on* these character traits rather than *be* them on the inside and then wonder why the results are not evident. Loving, authentic Christianity is not the witness. So why is this? God created you to *be* love and when you are not, there's no authenticity nor behaving from the core of who you were created to be.

Here's your example:

1. Jesus was and is love
2. Jesus loved

Jesus came from an unconditional, divine state of being so He could then love in human flesh. Then and only then, could He manifest in power, effect, and results. He chose to *be* love and is love. The difference is becoming love noun) on the inside instead of attempting to put it on and act loving on the outside when we aren't that on the inside. We attempt to be what we are not which is what Jesus came to change. Transformation is the process and freedom is the result. Free to be who we were created to be!

So, like Jesus, you are to live and *be*, powered by the choice to love and be love. Being love is by choice, intention, and commitment, empowered by His Holy Spirit. When you choose love and allow the Holy Spirit to guide you, you are your authentic self.

Remember, others live with you and maybe even more importantly, you live with yourself. The million-dollar question is, "How do you want to live with yourself?" Would you want to be the type of person who is open, calm, joyful, authentic, honest, and loving, or the opposite? If you want the former, you get to choose to follow the example Jesus gave us of unconditional, authentic love. Then abundant life can flow through you to others and this life can be true, pure, and lovely. When you are unconditional love, you are truly free.

Free to fly to the music of His joy,
Free to feel the waves tumble us in playfulness,
Free Choice—
The way it is meant to be.

THE HOLY SPIRIT

In this world, the war against good and evil is extremely evident. On one side is the good side, with peace and harmony. The other side is dark, which is evil. There is a call on the dark side to all who will hear to succumb to the pull of power, anger, death, and destruction. This evil pull is so strong that it separates families, friends, and even those in power.

God, in the person of the Holy Spirit, is a counselor and giver of knowledge and wisdom. God, in the person of the Holy Spirit, will come into your heart to be your guide and strength if you ask Him to! How this works will be covered throughout the rest of this book.

There are good and evil forces at work around you, ALL the time. You may or may not be aware of the evil temptations that pull you to do wrong things. To become a warrior of God, this work will support you in becoming more aware as well as increasing your connection with the Holy Spirit. You will learn how the Holy Spirit can guide you into all truth and warn you of danger, to list a few of the works He does!

As an example of how the Holy Spirit may talk to you, I will share an experience I had where the Holy Spirit gave me a gift of knowledge. At a church I was attending, I was on the prayer team. A lady wanted prayer and as I interviewed her, she told me why she needed prayer. While I prayed for what she wanted, the Holy Spirit and a still small voice inside of me kept impressing me to ask about her boyfriend. In obedience, I asked her about her boyfriend, and she was SHOCKED! "How did you know?" she asked. I said that God revealed this to me so she could be set free because He loved her. That night, she was set free when we prayed for her real need.

God works to free His people and the workers are few. That is why this book was written. This book is for those of you who are open to the light, want to live victoriously, and tell others the good news!

CONTENTS

As each part of A Way of Life can be purchased separately, some of the same writings are duplicated in some or each part of this book series. Examples include chapter 4 and, in the appendix, goal setting.

CHAPTER 1

TAKING STOCK: HUMILITY, HONESTY & FORGIVENESS

Review "MY Praise Song," found in the appendix.

My Praise Song talks about living and experiencing life freely. It talks about feeling pain and sorrow to fully appreciate and experience joy. Living fully human, fully alive. Are you doing that? This chapter will support this type of living and set you on a course to live life fully. Are you ready?

HUMILITY

Humility is an attitude of the mind requiring honesty. It is acknowledging the truth about yourself and not thinking more or less of yourself than who you are. If your understanding of humility is not what God teaches, it will affect your self-esteem negatively, which I don't think you want. Therefore, think about who and what God says you are (A child of the Most High God) and confess any unbelief about this truth.

Humility is also looking out for others and not demanding that you be served or get your own way. Philippians 2:7 says, "… rather, he made himself nothing by taking the very nature of a servant, being made in human likeness." (NIV) Jesus emptied Himself, which is your example to follow with an attitude of serving. It is neither self-centered nor self-conscious. Self-consciousness is an area where you may need healing. What would others think? How do I look? Am I accepted? Will others like me? The focus is on obtaining approval from others (man) rather than from God who views believers as His wonderful creation in Christ. As you look to understand others and yourself from God's perspective, humility begins to bloom.

HONESTY

Honesty is reality and truth according to the Word of God and acknowledging what is really happening inside you. Honesty is hindered whenever you do not face reality or how you feel as a fallible human being. Denial at times serves to protect you but also keeps you living a lie. Denial does not allow issues or emotions to be brought to light where God's principles and healing touch can help you. It is like wearing a pair of rose-colored glasses that prevent you from seeing reality. It is imperative that you seek to live honestly before God so that you can be set free. Ask for denial to be broken in your life and as you grow, God will make you as you were meant to be. God commands every believer to put away lying: "Let each one of you speak truth with his neighbor" (Ephesians 4:25). Just remember that you were created to be love and to speak the truth in love, which would improve many relationships on the block where you live!

FORGIVENESS

Why should you forgive? Because your life depends on it. Often, you might think that what another does is unforgivable—that the individual does not deserve to be forgiven. You may hold onto resentment and anger towards that person as a weapon against them. Are they aware of those feelings? Often not. Do they care? Likely not. The weapon of unforgiveness serves to destroy your relationship with God, your relationships with others, and with yourself. Negative feelings control you and although you might think you are in control, you are not. As tapes from the past play repeatedly in your mind, your mental health erodes. God says that He alone is the avenger—He will repay (Romans 12:19). I remember saying to myself as I was harboring ill will towards others, "I would not want to be around someone who was always feeling like this and here I am.... always around myself!" The point is that I chose not to hold onto any negative feelings. I did not want to live with *myself* that way. I wanted to walk God's way. It worked! Now, I live in peace! We all have a relationship with ourselves and the question to ask is: How do you want to live with yourself?

Giving others forgiveness does not mean that your hurt feelings are unjustified. You get to look beyond the hurt and anger and find the *reason* for the pain. Our growth is enabled through *experiencing, understanding, and speaking* about what has happened to us. Doing this also breaks the power that feelings have over us.

There is a lie that states, if you don't feel it, then it doesn't exist. Feelings exist whether you want them to or not. When you do not acknowledge these feelings, they still affect you, even on a subconscious level. Eventually, your reaction in a situation will stem from these unacknowledged feelings and usually, doesn't result in a positive event. However, if you earnestly pray for self-awareness, the Holy Spirit will support the understanding of your feelings. Psalm 44:21 says, "Would not God search this out? For He knows the secrets of the heart."

In forgiveness, it is important to look at the responsibility you might have played in allowing a situation to happen. Many people fail to take responsibility at this point and hence, are never totally free. Ask yourself, "Were my expectations too high? Were they unrealistic?" When you set unrealistic expectations for yourself and others, you fail and may blame yourself and/or others.

So, why forgive? Because God commands it. In the Lord's Prayer, there is a statement of concurrence (something happening at the same time); "forgive us our debts as we (same time as) forgive our debtors." Jesus went on to explain, "If you do not forgive men their trespasses, neither will your Father forgive your trespasses" (Matthew 6:15). Forgiveness does not mean that what happened was okay or that you are to continue being a doormat and getting hurt. It means that you choose not to be controlled by a root of bitterness, anger, or resentment that kills you from the inside out. With forgiveness comes peace and serenity. If you choose not to incorporate this principle into your life, then you are also choosing to disobey God. The consequence is turmoil, lack of peace, and separation from Him.

For those who do not know how to forgive, it starts with trying to understand your own shortcomings and humanity. As you openly acknowledge your sinful nature, the walls you might have built to protect yourself can fall and you can then begin to look at yourself and others with more understanding and compassion. This is loving yourself and others. Understand that there is a reason for all behavior. Perhaps others were never taught right from wrong as you were, growing up. You might think they "should" know how to treat others but, they may not. In that way, you place expectations on others and yourself that are not realistic.

I do think another command of, Know Yourself, would be beneficial so that you can understand and love yourself and others. Therefore, consider forgiving yourself a vital part of loving "you" as well as others in order to fulfill the second greatest commandment, "Love your neighbor *as you love* yourself." (Matthew 22:39)

MY SELF-EVALUATION

So, it's time to know yourself! Often, when individuals come up and compliment you, you might turn the blessing away. It is sometimes hard to recognize the good qualities that are in you. So, you get to practice! In this exercise, look for good things in yourself and notice if good things are hard for you to identify. Then list the challenges that you believe you have. To get you started, an example of strength is your willingness to learn and your commitment to going through this book. Challenge examples would be procrastinating on a project you've yet to finish or hesitancy in wanting to forgive others.

STRENGTHS	CHALLENGES

From here, writing a self-evaluation is a logical step. The purpose of writing a self-evaluation is an open admission of behaviors that hurt you or others. A self-evaluation is effective if you are honest with yourself and doing this can help free you from the guilt you have been carrying. It is best to write down everything, as this will clarify your thoughts and facilitate discovery. The questions below will support and guide you to write what is true for you. Please don't be afraid of exposing the truth to yourself and don't run and hide! No one will see this information unless you share it with them. Remember, the Holy Spirit is with you, so you are not alone!

God can help you write your self-evaluation. Psalm 139:1-2 states, "O Lord, You have searched me and known me. You know my sitting down and my rising up." Seek God's assistance and He will freely give it since depending on Him is His will for you. He made and knows you!

You might have difficulty writing your self-evaluation because you may fear God will not love you as He sees your challenges. Rest assured that God knows already, for "there is no creature hidden from His sight, but all things are naked and open to the eyes of Him to whom we must give account" (Hebrews 4:13). Yet, He still loves you. Remember, God "has reconciled us to Himself through Jesus Christ" (2 Corinthians 5:18). Therefore, as you bring things to the light, you are collaborating with God and His principles. God is so happy when you do this evaluation because He wants you to be free from anything weighing you down. He wants you to be free and work with you so you *are* free!

In your self-evaluation, you may feel that you hurt others because they first hurt you. The past is done but for the present and future, God says in Romans 12:17-19— "Repay no one evil for evil. Have regard for good things in the sight of all men. If it is possible, as much as depends on you, live peaceably with all men. Beloved, do not avenge yourself, but rather get rid of wrath; for it is written, Vengeance is Mine, I will repay, says the Lord."

What is God saying here about your response to others' actions or words against you?

What do you see that needs changing in your life to line up with what God is saying?

Denial has multiple faces including pretending, minimizing, blaming others, justifying behavior, and becoming angry to avoid an issue.

Where do you see denial being most active in your life?

List examples of when you have denied reality:

What anxieties do you have about your memories?

Resentments are damaging and cause great dis-ease and disease.

What is your major resentment and how is it interfering with your life?

List situations where you become angry because of the resentments you are holding onto:

List your major fear and how it is interfering with your life:

What fear surfaces when you realize God knows all your faults?

What is your major strength and how does it support you?

What is your major challenge and how does it hurt you?

List any resistance you may have in completing this self-evaluation:

Will this resistance serve you?

FIVE SAMPLE AREAS

The following are five different areas to support your self-evaluation with the Holy Spirit's help. As you work through each area, think about it for a couple of days before you start writing. Let the Spirit bring to remembrance what you can deal with right now. Do not agonize in trying to remember everything the first time through. You can do this again years from now and you will be surprised at what the Spirit will reveal that you had forgotten or is new!

AREA ONE: FAMILY RELATIONSHIPS

Write down below how your family members treated you and how you treated them. Were you close to them? Did anything hinder your intimacy as a family?

AREA TWO: SEXUAL CONSIDERATIONS

What were your first sexual experiences like? Were they before marriage? Multiple partners? Same-sex partners?

What did your family do to explain sexuality to you and talk to you about your sexuality?

Were you sexually abused and if so, by whom?

AREA THREE: AGES 0 – 12

Write down anything that stands out to you during these years. It could be good, such as playing soccer. It could be traumatic, such as being called names.

AREA FOUR: AGES 13 – 18

Write down anything that stands out to you during these years. It could be about dating, how you were accepted (or not) by your peers, how you felt about school, what your future plans were, your relationship with your parents, and your teaching regarding God at this point in your life.

AREA FIVE: AGE 18 – PRESENT

Write about any area that stands out, such as relationships that did not work and why you think they did not work. Additionally, write about lost dreams and emotional or sexual scars. Include any details you remember.

You have a choice to act on the following suggestion. Doing so will cause a release to occur in you as the hidden parts you have written about are brought to the light. The suggestion is to share what you have written with someone of the same sex that you trust. It could be a spouse or significant other if you know they will listen, not get upset about what you share or attempt to fix you.

Please review Chapter 2 before you share your self-evaluation with anyone. God will honor your courage in sharing your self-evaluation, so go with Him. His Spirit is always with you!

> Scripture to memorize this week: Psalm 51:1-4—
> "Have mercy on me, O God... Wash me thoroughly
> from my iniquity... My sin is always before me.
> Against You, You only, have I sinned..."

CHAPTER 2

CONFESSION

CONFESSION

In confession, you verbally bring to the light what was previously in darkness. You do not want to be on the dark side, where John 3:20 says, "Everyone practicing evil hates the light and does not come to the light, lest his deeds should be exposed." Proverbs 28:13 says, "He who covers his sins will not prosper, but whoever confesses and forsakes them will have mercy." Mercy means having a pass or not receiving the judgment due to us. Think of playing Monopoly and you get the free "Get Out of Jail" card. If you land on "Go to Jail," you get a pass. The above Proverb says that if you confess and forsake (turn away from) your wrongdoings, you get a pass from the judgment due you though you may suffer consequences. But, if you do not confess or turn away from your wrongdoings, you will not get a pass, you will be held accountable for them, and will continue to feel guilty.

Personally, I do not want to walk around feeling guilty all the time, so I don't! God knows my wrongs but still wants a relationship with me. When I speak to God and tell Him my wrongdoings, He meets me and heals my heart, my emotions, and creates a right spirit within me. I feel clean and clear of the fog and turmoil of my wrongs. He wants me to tell Him that I know I have done wrong and that I am sorry though I may still pay the consequences of my wrongdoing. It has been my life experience that when I confess my wrong, the consequences are not as terrible as they could have been if I had not confessed as soon as I became aware of what I was doing wrong.

God wants this type of relationship with you! God wants you to sincerely confess not only to Him but also to another person unless doing so would harm someone even more. Sometimes writing a letter and then burning it clears your emotions, your thinking, and the desire to retaliate or take revenge on another. You can feel lighter after you confess as it is a way of letting go of the past. Confession is one of God's principles for receiving mercy (the judgment that would have been due you) and living victoriously. You *cannot* live victoriously unless you incorporate this principle into your life. Ask the Holy Spirit and He will support you in incorporating this way of living into your walk with Him!

> **Scripture to memorize: Proverbs 28:13— *"He who covers his sins will not prosper, but whoever confesses and forsakes them will have mercy."***

SHARING YOUR SELF-EVALUATION

You might have already shared your self-evaluation with someone but if not, please keep these crucial factors in mind when deciding whom to share your self-evaluation with. It is advisable to choose someone of the same sex to be more open and comfortable sharing. Consider the following questions:

- Is the person trustworthy?
- Will they hold a confidence?
- How are their listening skills?
- Will they try to tell me what to do?
- Will they judge me as I share?
- Where do I want to hold this meeting?
- Will there be any distractions?
- What is the best time of day, so you won't be tired?

- Will they be able to hear and accept what I tell them?

As you meet with your confidant, openly discuss confidentiality, what you wish to gain from the meeting, and the expectations you have for the meeting. When you finish, share how you both experienced the sharing and what you have learned. If the sharing was not beneficial to you, please seek out a trusted, safe God-fearing mentor and talk to them about your experience and feelings.

When you finish sharing, take a moment to fill out the following questions.

What feelings did you have as you were sharing your evaluation?

Other than being relieved, how did you feel on the inside after this process was over?

How do you see God's principles healing you thus far?

What changes, if any, do you see in your behaviors, reactions, or attitudes during the time it took you to get to this chapter?

What benefit did you receive from completing this chapter?

CHAPTER 3

SANCTIFICATION &
BEING WILLING

SANCTIFICATION

Sanctification is the process of the continuing work of God in the life of a believer to make a person holy (more like Jesus). Sanctification can also be defined as being set apart, separate, or dedicated to a particular purpose or use. Being willing is a requirement for sanctification to work.

Sanctification will occur throughout your lifetime, leading you into a life of increasing purity and goodness. God does not expect you to be perfect although you may often expect that of others as well as yourself. He knew that you couldn't be perfect, so made provision for you through Jesus. Why, then, are you so hard on yourself and others? The grace, or unmerited favor you have received from God, allows you to stop trying to be perfect and be who you are. Allow the Holy Spirit to change you from the inside out to be loving and more like Jesus.

Sanctification will help you be more forgiving to yourself and others as your heart begins to understand and accept that we are all imperfect humans. Then, you can relax any expectations you have of yourself and others about acting in specific ways. What a refreshing thought!

Even though God does not expect you to be perfect, He does not give you or anyone the liberty to do as they please, believing they can just ask for forgiveness after the fact. Rather, knowing that you are imperfect and that His ways are always best, you can respond to His love and forgiveness by seeking to do His will for your life. You do this by dying daily, emotionally, spiritually, and laying aside your ego. Chapter 2 in Book 1 talks about how an absolutely surrendered will equals freedom. The focus is submitting yourself and being willing to hear what your Abba Father has to say in His word and through His Holy Spirit. Then, you get to hear or learn what action to take regarding what the Holy Spirit or God's word showed you. As you do the above, sanctification happens.

There was a period in my life when I was married to an unfaithful unbeliever. Our marriage was not good, and I didn't know what to do because I didn't believe in divorce. I believed that God could heal the marriage and felt that I was to be faithful to my vows no matter what my husband was doing. However, I knew that I needed to change any behavior that did not line up with God's Word and was hurtful to my marriage. I intentionally sought the Lord for two years to change me through prayer. I also went to women's groups to learn what God says about marriage and how to treat my husband. God began healing and changing my heart attitudes which made it easier to change my behaviors. Eventually, the time came when my husband got to choose whether he was committed or not and he chose to walk away. After my husband chose and left, I felt relief without guilt because I had worked to apply God's principles of living and loving my husband to fulfill my marriage vow. I sought the Lord and He met me in my time of need.

If you are facing any situation where you need an answer, sincerely and intentionally seek, knock, and ask the Lord. The answer will be found. It may not come in the timeframe that you want, but God promises that it will be found, in Matthew 7:7. This scripture says,

"Ask, and it will be given to you; seek, and you will find; knock, and it will be opened to you."

WILLINGNESS

Willingness is an attitude of openness to change. It is saying, "Yes, I will' versus "No, I can't." There is no such truth as "I can't" when it comes to the will. There is only, "I won't."

You may want to run from change but once you turn your thoughts away from the doubts and fears toward the issue or change at hand, your fear will lessen. Permitting yourself to be open to change, opens the door for the change to occur.

Willingness is the determination to do whatever it takes to make a change and accomplish your goals. It is a commitment to learning and understanding yourself, your world, and others. It is saying, "Yes, Lord, change me."

In this chapter, you are saying that you are willing for indwelling sin and sinful behaviors to be removed, not just lessened. God will respect your decision and move within you to free you if you ask Him to. He is asking you, as He did the man whom He healed by the pool in John 5:6, "Do you want to be made well?" You can choose to be made well and the appropriate feelings may not be immediately present but will follow. Did you hear that? Make decisions that are good for you whether you "feel" like it or not. The right feelings will line up. Also, the Holy Spirit is a gentleman and will not come into your heart and support you in your change if He is not welcomed and asked. He will not force you to do anything. The choice is yours.

Do you want to be made well?

What has God shown you that is to be removed, such as attitudes or heart motives?

Refer to your self-evaluation in Chapter 1 & write what you want to be gone that is lingering.

What are you not entirely ready to have removed?

What is stopping your willingness in these areas?

What purpose has whatever you are holding onto served in your life?

What will you willingly give up to be physically, mentally, or spiritually healthy?

What feelings do you have when you think about changing?

What behaviors have you tried in the past to change or fix within yourself and in your own power?

Whatever you are holding onto, how has that become part of your identity?

To become entirely ready (a new attitude), you have a choice. You have the choice to be willing to change how you react to people or situations in your life. Often, these patterns are so ingrained you may feel lost at the thought of them being absent or different. "Will anything take their place? Will I even exist, or will I feel dead?" you may ask. Be not afraid! If you draw close to God, new thoughts, new attitudes, and new patterns of following Christ will set you free! The Holy Spirit will gradually change you from the inside out as you take your wrong attitudes or actions to Him, confess them, and ask Him to forgive and change you.

Do you believe that God can uncover and remove those things that make you spiritually and emotionally sick?

Why or why not?

What does Paul state about God working in your life, found in Philippians 2:13? — *"It is God who works in you both to will and to do for His good pleasure."*

God says in Isaiah 41:10 — *"Fear not, for I am with you. Be not dismayed, for I am your God. I will strengthen you, yes, I will help you. I will uphold you with my righteous right hand."*

What does God say about any fear you may have about His working in your life?

Scripture also affirms, "Now this is the confidence that we have in Him, that if we ask anything according to His will, He hears us. And if we know that He hears us, whatever we ask, we know that we have the petitions that we have asked of Him" (1 John 5:14-15). It is God's will that you depend on Him for everything, as He states in Philippians 4:6, "Be anxious for nothing, but in everything by prayer and supplication, with thanksgiving, let your requests be made known to God." If you are sincerely depending on Him for your healing, then it follows that He will do it, for setting you free from continual sin is part of His plan and according to His will.

Do you believe that God will help you be free from your sin and become victorious?

Are you ready for Him to free you from your sin?

Answer yes in the following space if you have asked God to free you from what you want to be changed.

Ask God to change your will if your will won't conform to what He is telling you to do. God loves you and wants you to love Him and come to Him with everything. If you are sincere in your asking, act upon what He tells you to do and watch the results. The results may come gradually or fast but if you obey His Word and way, they will come.

Scripture to memorize this week: Psalm 51:2—
*"Wash me from my iniquity and cleanse me
from my sin."*

THE FACES WE HIDE BEHIND

To be whole as God intends you to be, become aware of your feelings so that they don't control you. Unawareness is a tool of Satan to keep you in bondage, but God has given you His Word "lest Satan should take advantage of us; for we are not ignorant of his devices" (2 Corinthians 2:11). If you aren't aware of your feelings, how can you take them to God and talk to Him about them? How can you understand and love yourself if you are unaware of who you are and how you feel?

You may have chosen to hide your fear, insecurity, and shame. The focus here will not be on the reasons you hide your feelings (these will be gently revealed through working with God, the Holy Spirit), but on learning what feelings you are hiding through the process of loving and understanding yourself. God made you, with all your precious feelings that give you information. It's important to become aware of them and bring them to God, knowing you are loved by Him and that you are safe with Him. If you sincerely want to know where the root of these feelings and the hiding of them comes from, He will begin to bring awareness to you about them. As you begin to love and understand yourself, the control these feelings have over you and the faces you hide behind will fade away.

Below, draw a picture of the face you have used most often to hide your feelings. For example, if you use cheerfulness, draw a smile. If you hide them through a deadpan (blank of emotions) face, draw that.

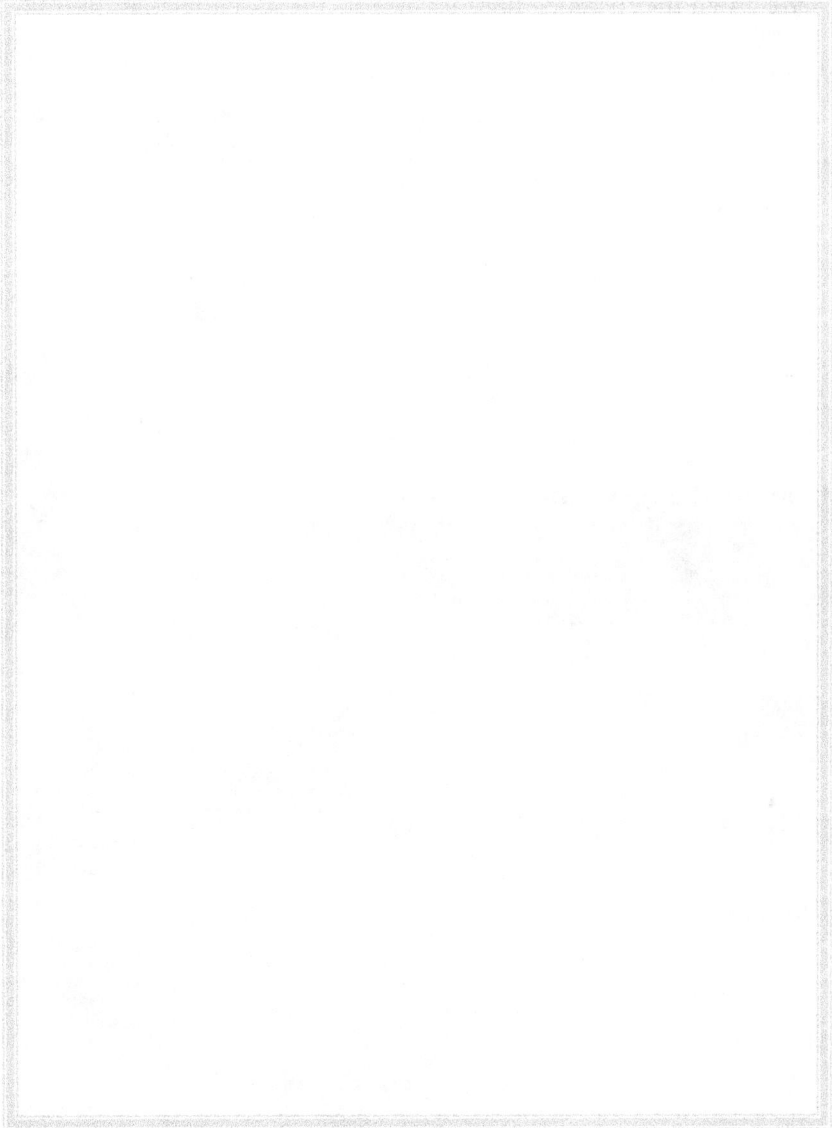

ABOUT ME

The following is an exercise to help you increase your awareness of your desires, feelings, and behavior. Once filled out, share what you have written with someone you trust. After you share with another, write down the feelings that you had during and after the sharing.

My hopes are:

I am most angry when:

I feel most sad when:

I run away from:

People I care for are:

I would describe myself as: (nouns and adjectives)

I feel most happy when:

My challenges are:

My strengths are:

Before sharing, I felt:

After sharing, I felt:

CHAPTER 4

SANCTIFICATION: PERSONAL GROWTH PLAN FOR ASSIMILATION & PRINCIPLE PRACTICE

Sanctification, according to Merriam-Webster, is defined as "the state of growing in divine grace as a result of Christian commitment after baptism or conversion." It is a growing in grace and our emphasis is on the word, growing. This is not a stagnant walk, nor is it boring! But it is worth it. 😊 This principle was covered earlier in this book but is covered again to look at applying the principles just reviewed.

I call a certain time in my life, baptism by fire. I was living in a marriage with my unfaithful husband and believed that God could change my marriage (which I do believe is the truth if BOTH parties are willing). So, I stayed in the marriage, hoping my husband would change his heart and mind. I knew that I was responsible for my part in the marriage, so began to pray that God would show me whatever I was doing wrong and change me. I asked God to create a clean heart in me and change my heart attitudes, motives, and behaviors.

I went to God daily and asked Him to have His Holy Spirit search me. He began to show me gently what needed to be changed and as a gentleman, heal and clean my heart and teach me His ways. As I read the bible, I began to see how relationships and God's universal principles work and I became grateful and thankful for what He was showing me.

Look in the Appendix for the Dependence on God wheel. These are the sanctification steps and the first one is being willing. Therefore, be sincere and willing to become aware of what doesn't line up with God's ways through reading His word. Ask Him to change what He shows you, on the inside, and do not resist the change. You'll be changing from the inside out (instead of trying to "put the change on") and the change will stick. Do whatever action He says to do and don't worry or be scared, even if what you are learning is painful to admit or you don't completely understand, yet. God is a gentleman and He will only collaborate with you to the point that you allow Him to. Do you want to be fully healed? Free from all your fears? Don't resist and seek the Lord. He will be with you 100% of the way. As you don't resist, you will gain as the following depicts:

"No pain, No gain."

These are the words the athletes sing
As they work their muscles to the sting.

"It hurts, it hurts," they cry
As the burning goes deeper and deeper into their thigh.

And yet they push on to never-ending fights,
Knowing that without this pain, they would never reach the heights.

And so, I say to you — you who so resist your pain —
Work it to the bone and do not deter,
For with your pain, you will gain.

—WHAT WE RESIST, PERSISTS—

PLAN

The intent of this book is the understanding and application of the information and principles covered, which is imperative for living victoriously. Below is a growth and development plan for you to solidify these life-giving principles in your life and all the lives that this work touches.

To create a personal growth development plan, start by defining what you've learned and what you want your results to be. Make sure you write them down. Next, perform a self-assessment and identify one area that needs attention. Then, determine the required actions and develop an action plan using the "SMARTER" goal-setting method, found in the appendix.

Here is an example of a growth plan.

What I want: To be effective as a leader of my family and at work.

What I do now:	What I learned:	What I will change:	The time period to practice my change:	The outcome:
I tend to control others and situations. I don't listen and make collaborative decisions with others.	I learned that surrendering frees me to be me. and that I don't have control over others. I only can control myself.	Listen with my heart before I speak. Listen for the truth and work with it only.	By the end of the next month.	1. My coworkers and family will notice and say something. 2. I will feel open on the inside rather than stressed and closed off.

Implement with goals: (see appendix on how to set goals)

Example of a SMARTER goal with its supporting activities to reach the stated goal. The scale used is from 1-10 with 10 being high.

Goal: By the end of next month, my family and coworker will see me as an effective leader as evidenced by them saying something about my behavior change and I will have a stress score reduction from an 8 to a 4 by the end of next month.

Simple:	yes
Measurable:	stress score lower, family/coworkers will say something about my behavior change
Achievable:	this is achievable
Realistic:	this is realistic
Timely:	end of the next month
Evaluate goal:	end of next month and stress level reduction level
Reset goal:	change it, extend the end time, or create another goal

Activities:

1. For the next month, at work and in every meeting, I will not be the first to speak and share my opinion. I will share...just not first!

2. For the next month, I will listen with my heart to what my family says and seek to understand their perspective before stating mine. I will do that by asking questions.

Now, it's your turn!

On a separate piece of paper that you can hang where you will see it frequently, type or write out your growth plan to assimilate and apply the principles you just learned. Find a safe friend who will listen and share your plan with them and as someone I know says, "git'r done!"

CONCLUSION

As A Way of Life, in its full workbook format, was so meaty, I was advised to divide the work into multiple small courses. Therefore, I have divided A Way of Life, Kingdom Principles for Living Victoriously, into 4 parts and this concludes book 2. There is much more that leads to peace within and I want to encourage you to continue learning and applying God's principles so that you *will* experience freedom and peace within.

To continue your journey & in your internet browser, type in AWayofLifeMinistries.com. Click on the Bookstore or Courses tab to find resources and purchase whatever you need to continue your journey and growth. You can also search on Amazon for A Way of Life by Nancy Williams to purchase from there.

Please let us know how your journey is going by using the Contact Us form on the website to connect with us. We would LOVE to hear from you about how you are progressing. You can also subscribe to our blog page and we'll keep you informed of upcoming events, new publications, online courses, and book offerings. Hope to hear from you soon and if you have questions, please ask!

Blessings on your journey
~ Nancy ~

SUGGESTED READING LIST

The following 4 books are secular but may be helpful. Read them with caution and a biblically discerning mind.

- Beattie, Melody. (1987). Codependent No More. New York: Harper & Row.

- Bradshaw, John. (1988). The Family. Florida: Health Communications, Inc.

- Fromm, Erich. (1956). The Art of Loving. New York: Harper & Row.

- Peck, M. Scott, MD. (1978). The Road Less Traveled. NY: Simon & Schuster, Inc.

The following list is from a Christian perspective. I encourage you to read especially Francis Schaeffer's, True Spirituality, R.A. Torry's, The Person and Work of the Holy Spirit, and J. Keith Miller's, A Hunger for Healing.

- Bennett, Dennis and Rita. (1971). The Holy Spirit and You. New Jersey: Logos International.

- Bridges, Jerry. (1978). The Pursuit of Holiness. Colorado: Navpress.

- Bridges, Jerry. (1983). The Practice of Godliness. Colorado: Navpress.

- Buhler, Rich. (1988). Pain and Pretending. Tennessee: Thomas Nelson, Inc.

- Esses, Michael. (1974). The Phenomenon of Obedience. New Jersey: Logos Int.

- Huggett, Joyce. (1986). The Joy of Listening to God. Illinois: InterVarsity Press.

- Miller, J. Keith. (1991). A Hunger for Healing. New York: Harper Collins.

- Powell, John. (1969). Why Am I Afraid to Tell You Who I Am? Illinois: Argus Comm.

- Powell, John. (1974). The Secret of Staying in Love. Texas: Argus Communications.

- Powell, John. (1976). Fully Human, Fully Alive. Illinois: Argus Communications.

- Powell, John. (1978). Unconditional Love. Texas: Argus Communications.

- Schaeffer, Francis A. (1971). True Spirituality. Illinois: Tyndale House Publishers.

- Seamands, David A. (1981). Healing for Damaged Emotions. Illinois: SP Pub., Inc.

- Smalley, Gary and Trent, John, Ph.D. (1986), The Blessing. Tennessee: Thomas Nelson, Inc.

- Smith, Chuck. (1979,1980). Effective Prayer Life. California: The Word For Today.

- Swindoll, Charles R. (1983). Dropping Your Guard. New York: Bantam Books.

- Torrey, R.A. (1974). The Person & Work of the Holy Spirit (rev. ed.). Michigan: Zondervan Publishing House.

- Watson, David. (1980). The Hidden Battle. Illinois: Harold Shaw Publishers.

- Whitfield, Charles L., M.D. (1987). Healing the Child Within. Florida: Health Comm., Inc.

- Wilkerson, David; and Sherrill, John & Elizabeth. (1963). The Cross and The Switchblade. New Jersey: Spire Books.

APPENDIX

It is recommended to review and use all the resources in this appendix to continue your growth journey and find your blessings as you do so.

USING A WAY OF LIFE
IN GROUP SETTINGS

This book has been used in multiple group settings, so the below has been included to support group success and encourage individuals to be facilitators. Usually, there is sharing of what God is doing in each person and what spoke to them from the chapter being reviewed.

GROUP LEADERS

Ground Rules, which are to be read to the small group:

- Confidentiality is of utmost importance
- Please don't put down another's person, thoughts, or opinions—each person is of equal value
- It's OK to say that you don't want to share
- Please share time equally. Give everyone a chance to share
- One person talks at a time
- Please be personal. Use "I" or "me" statements
- We work together as a team
- Talk from feelings, not stories or circumstances
- Don't give advice
- Listen and try to understand what is being said

Good Family Functional Rules are taken from Bradshaw on: The Family by John Bradshaw. Copyright 1988. Health Communications, Inc. Used with permission from the author and if used in the group, the group will be healthy. Facilitators are to read the following Functional Rules at the beginning of each group.

- Problems are acknowledged and resolved
- 5 freedoms—can be expressed and explored with no judgment
  - ✓ perceptions
  - ✓ feelings
  - ✓ thoughts
  - ✓ desires
  - ✓ fantasies
- Communication is direct, specific, and behavioral
- Family members get their needs met
- Family members can be different
- Parents do what they say (self-disciplined disciplinarians)
- Atmosphere is fun and spontaneous
- The rules require accountability
- Violation of another's values leads to guilt
- Mistakes are forgiven and viewed as learning tools
- Individuals are in touch with their healthy shame
- The family systems exist for each other
- What to discuss in the group setting:
- What was particularly meaningful to you from the last chapter?
- How do you see this affecting your life right now?
- Are there any changes that you want to make?

Closing in Prayer: What can we pray about tonight or during this coming week?

DEPENDENCE ON GOD

S ee below, where God is in the middle and all the spokes have their focus on Him and His way. Walk through steps 1-11 in order and watch the results within yourself! The result is having the change desired.

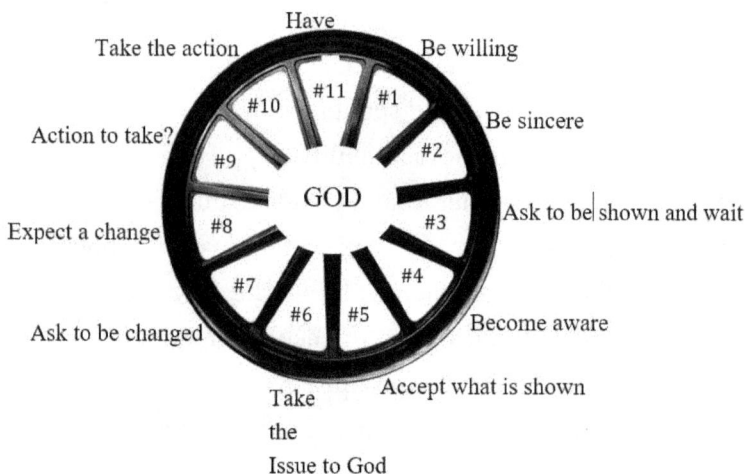

The beginning of your dependence on God starts with your being willing, and goes until you BE, DO, and then Have, regarding each situation. Be willing & sincere, ask to be shown, and God will open your heart and you will begin to be aware of what you get to know. Accepting this knowledge is critical to your personal & spiritual growth. Take what God shows you back to Him and ask for it and for you to be changed. Expect Him to work within you and you will know when things are changing. He may show you some action to take, so make sure you complete the action and you will be closer to being or having what He wants you to be or have.

This cycle works for everything and while most elements are important, being willing and sincere to ask to be shown what needs to be changed, or ask for understanding, etc. is most important. If you are not sincere or willing, this cycle of growth and understanding will not work.

Point # 1	You are WILLING
Point # 2	You are SINCERE
Point # 3	You ASK TO BE SHOWN
Point # 4	You are AWARE
Point # 5	You ACCEPT WHAT WE ARE SHOWN
Point # 6	You TAKE THE ISSUE TO GOD
Point # 7	You ASK TO BE CHANGED
Point # 8	You EXPECT A CHANGE
Point # 9	You look for what ACTION TO TAKE
Point # 10	You TAKE THE ACTION
Point # 11	You BE, DO, then HAVE

To refresh the understanding of what is meant by the BE—DO—HAVE statement, refer to the introduction at the beginning of this book. Then, enjoy and experience the newfound freedom that God gives to you as you submit and depend on Him!

MY PRAISE SONG

My pain is real. It hurts. At times, I feel as if I am dead inside. Other times I feel as if my heart is breaking into pieces. But—I have come to appreciate my pain for what it teaches me.

I feel solid inside when I acknowledge my pain, which is a special feeling for me. Far too often in the past, I have been tossed to and fro, not wanting to feel my sorrow. I cheated myself of feeling the depth to which my pain goes.

BUT NO MORE

I grow as I experience and **listen** to my pain. Movement happens within me without my even trying to make it happen. My path becomes clearer before me as I **walk with** my pain rather than around it.

BUT THERE IS MORE

I have learned that without knowing my pain and sorrow, I cannot fully appreciate and experience the joy that is within me. I have also come to see that as I acknowledge all that is within me, I am experiencing life and living the woman GOD made me to be. When I die, I will know that I have lived life to the fullest: That I have loved well, cried well, and have lived fully human, fully alive.

THIS IS MY PRAISE SONG

I want to acknowledge John Powell's book, Fully Human, Fully Alive, which greatly impacted me at an early age.

PERFECT LOVE

Everyone longs to give himself or herself completely to someone: To have a deep, soul relationship with another, to be loved thoroughly and exclusively. But to you, Christian, I say no. Not until you're satisfied and fulfilled and content with being loved by Me alone and giving yourself totally and unreservedly to Me in an intensely personal and unique relationship with Me. I love you, My child, and until you discover that only in Me is your fullest satisfaction to be found, you will not be capable of the perfect human relationship that I have planned for you.

You will never be united with another until you are united with Me, exclusive of any other desires or longings. I want you to stop planning, stop wishing, and allow Me to bless you in My time. You just keep watching Me, expecting the greatest things. Keep learning and listening to the things I tell you. You must wait.

Don't be anxious, looking around at the things you think you want. Just keep looking up to Me, or you'll miss what I have to show you.

Then, when you're ready, I'll surprise you with a love far more wonderful than any you would ever dream of. You see, until you are ready and until the one I have for you is ready, I am working this minute to have both of you ready at the same time and until you are both satisfied exclusively with Me and the life I've prepared for you, you won't be able to experience the perfect love that exemplifies your relationship with Me.

And dear one, I want you to have this most wonderful love. I want you to personally experience a picture of your relationship with Me, enjoying materially and concretely the everlasting union of beauty, perfection, and love that I offer you with Myself. Know that I love you with an everlasting love. I am God Almighty; believe and be satisfied.

Always,

Your Heavenly Father

CONFRONTATION AND COMMUNICATION

onfrontation is not an ugly word!

The Apostle Paul explained to the Ephesian church, "All things that are exposed are made manifest by the light, for whatever makes manifest is light" (Ephesians 5:13). The Word of God is your source of light. God's principles are there to guide you in how to interact with your fellow human beings, separating truth from error. He gives you His Holy Spirit to support you in discerning the truth from the lie.

Confrontation is not an ugly word. It can be used to set God's people free when the truth is spoken in love. You can be set free yourself by standing on the truth and speaking it. Denial can be broken. To deny, individuals are required to be dishonest. Satan would love for the fog in your mind to become increasingly thick. Then, you will have a hard time hearing God OR seeing Him move in your life. Denial is a sin that most individuals don't consider it being. You likely use it to protect yourself for one reason or another, but it is time to put to death that method of hiding from others and yourself and bring all aspects of your life to the light of God's Word. Confrontation is speaking the truth, or what you perceive to be the truth until the full picture is known (knowing that you may not have all the facts available to you). It is bringing what was hidden to the light. It is a way of working with others, being sensitive to them as fellow creatures of God, as you verbalize the truth. The Holy Spirit is your guide for sensitivity regarding if, when, and how you are to speak.

Motives are to be evaluated before any confrontation with another. Operating in anger or revenge is not following the principles of God. An attitude of looking for the best and desiring for the truth to reign gracefully is a must in how you interact with another. Our MOTIVE must be one of LOVE.

Communication is an art. It is active listening, coupled with discernment and sensitivity. Active listening is tuning into the actual words, as well as any underlying messages (undercurrents) that your senses may pick up. Individuals may say they are fine but are not. What they usually want is for you (or someone else) to take the initiative to ask them what is wrong. If that occurs, a need is met. If not, the individual goes away feeling as if no one cares about them, which is a lie. Additionally, they didn't speak up either. Was there truthful communication there? No, and this occurs frequently in relationships. You may expect other individuals to read your mind and when they don't, you may blame them for not meeting your needs. Who is really to blame? If you act this way, you are to blame because you were not clear in communicating your needs. That is why WORDS and HOW WE USE THEM are so important. "Death and life are in the power of the tongue and those who love it will eat its fruit" (Proverbs 18:21). One of those fruits is bridging the gap between separation and intimacy through godly communication. Remember, be kind, direct and clear.

Thoughtful questioning is another ingredient in the confrontation and communication process to clarify what is heard. What one individual means with a word may be different from your perception of that word. Clarify so you both can be sure you are talking the same language. Have you ever walked away from a conversation feeling uncertain about what was decided? Avoid that by being direct and clear.

Write down an example of a sensitive issue that you talked over with someone:

Do you feel that you had the issue/s clearly defined in your mind before the conversation?

What was your attitude before the communication?

Do you feel that what you were trying to communicate was done clearly or vaguely?

What was good about how the communication worked out?

What could have been improved?

How did you feel before you began talking?

How did you feel after the conversation was over?

Do you feel that the truth was established?

Why or why not?

In communication that requires confrontation, how others respond to your communication is not the issue. God calls you to be honest and righteous before Him. If your heart is pure before Him, as you communicate necessary and/or difficult issues with another person, the other's response is up to them as they stand before God. You are responsible only for your actions and attitudes. How the other person responds is their responsibility before God and there will be times when confrontation works wonderfully well and intimacy is established. How joyful are those times! However, there will be times of sorrow and confusion when difficult conversations do not end well. Add this to the fact that people communicate differently and sometimes, words sound like Greek to each other! Evaluate your part in why the outcome happened the way that it did and learn from your mistakes. God loves you just the way you are, but because of His love for you, He doesn't want you to stay there. He wants to transform you to be like Him and will use even difficult conversations to help bring that about.

HOW WE LEARN AND COMMUNICATE

Y ou fall into one or two (dominant for you) categories of learning and communicating. As you seek to relate well to one another, it is helpful to be aware of how you and those you are communicating with learn or hear best. You can then learn to talk in their "language." The description of each separate category concludes with examples to enhance our ability to communicate with this type of learner.

VISUAL:

This person learns and communicates best through sight. Using word pictures helps get the message across to others using sight words. This is drawing with words, a visual illustration of what you are trying to say. Using words such as watch, look, gaze, reflect, see, and show tap into this sight activity. (We will consider this further in a separate section)

Examples:

"I see what you mean."

"It looks OK to me."

"This appears to be right to me."

AUDITORY:

This person learns and communicates best through hearing. You can identify an auditory learner by the words he or she uses such as hear, say, sound, talk, tell, and explain. When communicating with an auditory learner, use hearing words.

Examples:

"Do you hear what I am saying?"

"Let me tell you."

"Does that ring a bell?"

"It sounds interesting to me."

KINESTHETIC:

This person learns and communicates best through being able to touch, taste, smell, chew, hold, and feel things. He or she learns best through experience. A kinesthetic learner is likely to use words such as build, feel, catch, do, grasp, hold, make, shape, and touch, so use these words to capture their attention.

Examples:

"That feels good to me."

"I think I can grasp that."

The following example shows the difference in language between the three categories:

Visual:	"That looks good to me."
Auditory:	"That sounds good to me."
Kinesthetic:	"That feels good to me."

You operate in all three categories, but you normally favor one category above the rest. Knowing how you and those closest to you tend to communicate will promote peaceful relationships as you talk to them in their favorite learning and communication language!

COMMUNICATION

The following depicts key elements of the communication process. They are given in outline fashion to make it easy for you to review them often, for the more you understand and practice them, the more your communication with others will improve.

Communicate with purpose:

- Influence behavior/ideas/thoughts
- Convey information
- Build relationships

Before communicating, ask yourself if your purpose is to confront, resolve an issue, or share since the way you approach speaking will differ. Remember a key biblical concept: Philippians 2:3— "Let nothing be done through selfish ambition or conceit, but in lowliness of mind let each esteem others better than himself." Applying that scripture to your attitude and heart as you communicate will support your awareness of how words may be perceived by others and how that affects their feelings.

Ways of communicating:

- Linear-----one sided

    Person A sends a message to Person B

    (sender------->--------->receiver)

- Circular

    Person A sends a message to B and B responds. Feedback happens

    Sender A <------------->B receiver and then B sends a communication back to the sender. Communication doesn't continue. Example: A: How are you? B: I'm fine

- Mutual transaction

    Person A sends a message to B and B responds. A then responds

    A----->B----->A----->B

    Feedback happens both ways with increased emotional relating (both influence the other)

You as a sender:

- Must be clear in the message sent
- Responsible to evaluate the *words used to send the message* and if what was said was exactly what you wanted to send

You as a receiver:

- Responsible to understand that you *hear through your perception filter*, which can result in a *different message heard than what was sent*

- You are responsible for verifying that what you heard is what was sent, by the sender

Be aware that receivers can have preconceived ideas of the sender, which will cloud communication. The mutual transaction helps ensure that what was said was heard correctly. *Verifying that what you received is what was meant to be sent is the key to preventing misunderstandings and assumptions.*

Non-verbal communication:

Non-verbal communication comprises about 55 percent of the communication process. The rest of the breakdown is 7 percent verbal and 38 percent vocal, with inconsistencies in what you say and do frequently occurring.

In Non-verbal communication:

a. Our 5 senses are used: Sight, hearing, smell, taste, touch
b. 4 categories

- Kinesics—your body movements, facial expressions, body language, clothes
- Tactile—who can touch whom, when and how
- Paralanguage—how your voice is when speaking (tone—which includes the force of your voice; if your voice is relaxed or edgy, etc.)
- Proxemics
  - Use of physical/personal space
  - Who can come in and when
  - Distance
    - public—no personal contact
    - social—4-12 feet
    - personal—1½ -4 feet
    - intimate—6"-18"

c. More feelings are communicated non-verbally than verbally

Factors affecting how communication is perceived:

a. Our mood
b. Preconceived notions of the speaker and the topic being spoken about (selective hearing)
c. Mental level of the person being spoken to

Evaluating your communication:

a. Speaker—primary responsibility to get ideas across
    - Emotions can cloud the words used
    - Emotions cloud the way words are used
    - Push past emotion, speak accurately, and lovingly
    - Stay focused and avoid distractions

b. Hearer—keep in mind:
    - Distractions
    - Vocabulary and language skills
    - Wishful hearing
    - Perception filter

c. Things to avoid in your communication:
    - Using clichés
    - Giving unwanted advice or approval
    - Belittling speech or actions
    - Disagreeably disagreeing
    - Being defensive
    - Stereotyping and over-generalizing
    - Changing the subject before resolution such as bringing up other topics that don't relate and can throw off the focus (if allowed) of the topic being discussed
    - Blaming
    - Responding with anger and hostility—Proverbs 17:14 says, "The beginning of strife is like a releasing [a flood]. Therefore, stop contention before a quarrel starts."
    - Raising more than one issue at a time
    - Judging (condemning) —Matthew 7:2— "With what judgment you judge, you will be judged."

Tools for excellent, honest communication:

a. Active listening—we speak about 125 words per minute but think about 4 times as fast

- Demonstrate understanding and respect for the speaker's message and feelings
- Be empathetic and sympathetic
- Concentrate on the speaker's perspective
- Is not casual—takes energy
- Is not parroting back words, but using open-ended questions, such as, "Can you give me an example?"
- Is a priority: James 1:19 says, "Let every man be swift to hear, slow to speak, slow to wrath."

b. Considerate speaking:

- Raise only one issue at a time
- "Be kind to one another, tenderhearted to one another, just as God in Christ forgave you" (Ephesians 4:32)
- "A soft answer turns away wrath, but a harsh word stirs up anger" (Proverbs 15:1)
- Proverbs 16:21 says, "The wise in heart will be called prudent and sweetness of the lips increases learning."

c. Clarification:

- Attempt to understand
- *Validate what a person is saying*
- Focus
- *Summarize to make sure what was said was indeed heard*

d. Be aware of others and your nonverbal body language (see following pages)

e. Follow the speaker. What this means is to listen to the whole story. Don't judge or tune out as you may miss an important idea, a person's heart, their point, or something about the person sharing. Jesus told His disciples to follow and learn of Him; to learn of His perspective. With an open mind and listening skills, you can walk alongside others, learn their perspective, and love them

Concluding scriptural consideration:

Philippians 4:8 says to meditate on whatever is:

- True
- Noble
- Just
- Pure
- Lovely
- Of good reputation (or good report)
- Virtuous
- Praiseworthy

God calls you to cultivate an attitude of thinking the best for all and facilitating the best in all. Your flesh wants you to assume the worst, even though the worst may not exist except in your own mind because of your past. God calls you not to think on the worst but on the best, so training your mind is an ongoing task.

Non-verbal behavioral components:

Type	Aggressive	Assertive	Passive
Eye contact	Stares, glares	Looks in eves	Avoids eves
Posture	Exaggerated, rigid	Open, upright	Slumped, head down
Gestures	Tightly clenched fist, points finger	Relaxed, expressive	Fidgeting hands
Distance	Intrusive	Comfortable	Moves away
Verbal loudness	Louder than normal range	Normal range	Softer than normal range
Tone of voice	Harsh	Clear	Clear to sing-song/whiny
Style/ fluency	Offensive, bombastic	Direct, smooth	Indirect, interrupts
Content	Derogatory put-downs	To the point, brief	Wordy, indirect
Listening	Interrupts and is closed to other's viewpoint	Doesn't interrupt when others speak. Listens to others' viewpoint, open	The tendency is to partially listen to what is said & often misinterprets

Basics of good communication:

   a.   Active listening

   b.   Open questioning

   c.   Accepting and reflecting on feelings

Activity	Examples of Activity
Active Listening: Convey interest in what the other person is saying. Encourage the other to expand further	Smiling, nodding, eye contact, "I see", "uh-huh" "Yes, go on," "Tell me more," "I'd like to hear more"
Open Questioning: Help the other clarify the problem in their thinking. Help the other hear what they have said, in the way it sounded to you. Pull out the key ideas	"Then the problem as you see it is that..." "If I understand you correctly, you are saying that..." "Your major concern is..."
Accepting and reflecting feelings: Respond to the other's feelings more than their words	"You feel strongly that..."

Offering constructive compliments:

- Be specific—focus on behavior or incident
- Be direct
- Compliment in public
- Compliment often but be sincere and sensitive

Offering constructive criticism:

- Be specific—focus on the behavior or incident
- Be sure the behavior you are criticizing can be changed
- Talk from your point of view and avoid threats and accusations
- Don't belabor the point

- Offer incentives for changed behavior and commit yourself to share in resolving the situation
- Empathize with the other's problem or feelings
- Choose an appropriate time and place

Accepting compliments:

- Say thank you!

Accepting criticism:

- Think of it as a source of new information to be evaluated objectively
- Channel the emotional energy aroused by criticism into fruitful avenues
- Take the necessary steps to put behavioral changes into action

The above talks about how to create excellent communication, regardless of how the other responds. Our responsibility is how we communicate. How the other person we are communicating with communicates back is not our responsibility and we get to separate ourselves to that truth. In other words, don't REACT back if the other person is not responding in the same manner as what you are learning. It takes time but the more we do our responsibility and not attempt to control the outcome, the more excellent our communications will be, regardless of how a person responds.

There are three books I would like to recommend in support of improving your communication style. The information for these books is found in the appendix and they are:

1. Boundaries, by Henry Cloud and J. Townsend
2. Am I Making Myself Clear, by Terry Felber
3. The 16 Undeniable Laws of Communication, by John C. Maxwell

Word Pictures is the next subject and learning how to create word pictures will support becoming an excellent communicator with those you love and those around you.

WORD PICTURES

The following was borrowed from the book, The Language of Love, by Gary Smalley and John Trent, Ph.D., and published by Focus on the Family. © 1988. All rights reserved. International copyright secured. Used by permission from Focus on the Family. It is recommended to purchase this book and study it to increase your communication tool belt. 😊

What word pictures are:

Word pictures are a communication tool that uses a story or object to simultaneously activate the emotions and intellect of a person. This, in turn, causes a person to **experience** your words, not just hear them. The **impact** of your words is **multiplied**. The word picture usually does not have a literal meaning. It's like a coloring book in words.

Reasons why word pictures work:

a. Time-tested (used as examples) by the world's greatest communicators

- Aristotle— "He entered combat in body like the strongest bull, in spirit like the fiercest lion."
- Churchill— "Dictators may walk to and fro among tigers, but they dare not be deceived. The tigers are getting hungry, too." (Cautionary note regarding word pictures: Dictators use them too, so beware of the motive of the speaker)

- Martin Luther King, Jr.— "Let us not seek to satisfy our thirst for freedom by drinking from the cup of bitterness and hatred."
- Excerpts from the Bible—Psalm 23 and the Good Shepherd, Luke 10 and the Good Samaritan

b. Grabs and directs attention (first 30 seconds is most important)

- You only have a few seconds to get someone's attention. An example: We don't drive cars—we drive Mustangs, Broncos
- Your brain works faster with pictures than listening to conventional words, which promotes straining to see what lies behind the story

c. Brings the message to life

- Activates emotions that can produce a positive change in a person's thinking
- Creates a theater of the mind or mental journey
- Can be physically affecting, triggering all 5 senses

d. Locks thoughts into our memory: not a lost memory, but a lasting memory

e. Gateway to intimacy

- Bridges the gap between the different ways of thinking between men and women
- Women use 25,000 words/day; women tell the story first, then facts. Telling the story first helps a woman attempt to get a man to feel and hear her words and maximizes her innate relational abilities
- Men use 12,500 words/day; men want facts first, then the story

How to create a word picture:

a. Establish clear purposes, such as to:
- Motivate godly and noble actions
- Clarify thoughts and feelings
- Move to a deeper intimacy level
- Praise or encourage someone
- Lovingly correct someone

b. Study the other person's interest
- David—shepherd/defender word pictures
- Paul—athlete/laborer word pictures

c. Draw from the following 4 inexhaustible wells
- Nature and its wonders—e.g., woods, birds
- Everyday objects—e.g., leftovers, flags
- Imaginary stories—can be memorable, e.g., Narnia, Middle Earth
- Past experiences and remembrances—a direct path to a person's emotions

d. Rehearse your story

e. Give the word picture at the right time and place

The value of using word pictures in the home:

a. Security—creates a warm blanket of love in the heart
- Score with family members from 1-10 on how secure their heart feels by love and feeling heard. A score of 1 would not be very secure and a 10 score would be very secure
- Discern what it would take to move closer or maintain a higher security level
- Use word pictures to strengthen the self-esteem of each family member

b. Meaningful communication—heart-to-heart praise, discipline, & love

c. Psalm 128 family word picture: "Blessed is everyone who fears the Lord, who walks in His ways. When you eat the labor of your hands, you shall be happy and it shall be well with you. Your wife shall be like a fruitful vine in the very heart of your house, your children like olive plants all around your table. Behold, thus shall the man be blessed who fears the Lord" (vv.1-4)

LISTENING AND UNDERSTANDING

Listen to understand:

- Love looks to understand
- Understanding promotes love and intimacy
- Promote an attitude of looking for the truth to listen and understand
- With knowledge comes understanding

Proverbs on understanding:

Proverbs 2:2-3 states — *"Incline your ear to wisdom, and apply your heart to understanding; yes, if you cry out for discernment, and lift up your voice for understanding ...then you will understand the fear of the Lord and find the knowledge of God."*

Proverbs 4:5 — *"Get wisdom! Get understanding!"*

Proverbs 13:15-16 — *"Good understanding gains favor.... Every prudent man acts with knowledge, but a fool lays open his folly."*

Proverbs 16:22 — *"Understanding is a wellspring of life to him who has it."*

Proverbs on speaking the truth:

> Proverbs 12:17,22 — *"He who speaks truth declares righteousness. ...Those who deal truthfully are His delight."*

> Proverbs 15:28 — *"The heart of the righteous studies how to answer, but the mouth of the wicked pours forth evil."*

A blessing for the listener:

- With your ears, may you hear each word as something very precious
- With your mind, may you humbly search to understand
- With your eyes, may you note the non-verbal message
- With your heart, may you listen with real love
- And may your hearing, understanding, and love be as lasting and enduring as a precious stone

PLEASE HEAR WHAT
I'M NOT SAYING

Don't be fooled by the face I wear, for I wear a mask. I wear many masks; masks I'm afraid to take off and none of them are I.

Pretending is an art that is second nature to me, but don't be fooled. I give you the impression I am secure. That confidence is my name and coolness is my game. That the water is calm and I'm in command needing no one. But—please don't believe that.

My surface may be smooth, but my surface is my mask. Beneath dwells the real me, in confusion, fear, and aloneness. But I hide that. I don't want anyone to know it. I panic at the thought of my weakness and fear being exposed. That's why I frantically create a mask to hide behind: a nonchalant, sophisticated facade to help me pretend, to shield me from the glance that knows. But—such a glance is my only salvation and I know it. That is if it is followed by acceptance and love. It is the only thing that can liberate me from myself, from the barriers I so painstakingly erect. It is the only thing that will assure me of what I can't assure myself: that I really am worth something.

I'd really like to be genuine, but please help me. Please hold out your hands, even when that's the last thing I seem to want or need. Only you can call me into being alive. Each time you're kind, gentle and encouraging: each time you try to understand because you really care, you breathe life into me. I want you to know that. I want you to know how important you are to me. You can support the creation of the person I am becoming if you choose to. You can help break down the wall behind which I tremble. You can help release me from the lonely prison of panic and insecurity.

Please don't pass me by. It will not be easy. A long-time conviction of worthlessness builds strong walls. The nearer you approach me, the more likely I will strike back. I know it's irrational, but at times, I am irrational. I fight against the very thing I cry out for, which is to be heard, known, and loved. But I am told that love is stronger than strong walls and there lies my hope—my only hope.

Please break down these walls with gentle hands, for I am very sensitive. Who am I? I am someone you know very well: I am every person you'll ever meet.

Anonymous

GOAL SETTING

Many individuals have never been taught about goal setting. This exercise will teach you how to clearly state your goals and then set up subgoals (activities) to achieve them.

First—why should you set goals? Isn't God supposed to do everything for you? He can intervene and move you where He wants you to be, can't He? So, why do you have to do anything?

Yes, God can move you if He so desires to work that way. Most often, He doesn't. He can speak to you, but it is up to you to function as His vessel here on earth. Setting goals can be for any part of your life—for what God has spoken to your heart for you to do, for your growth, education, or fun.

When goals are set, there's something that will arise in you to begin working to complete the goal. A purpose will grow within you and just skimming along in life doing who knows what, ends. Goals don't have to be great feats, but as you begin setting goals and moving forward, God directs your path. You can direct a moving car, but not a parked one. Goals help you get moving!

Think of the term SMARTER to support you in writing your goals:

        Specific (make it simple and clear)

        Measurable

        Achievable

        Realistic

Timely

Evaluate

Reset goal

Sample goal:

I will study my Bible 4 times a week for 1 hour over a one-month period, in June.

S:	personal Bible study
M:	4 times/week
A:	clearly stated
R:	can be achieved
T:	over a month's time (specify which month)
E:	to be done after a month or throughout the month
R:	select another month or pick different Bible-study goals

Subgoals (or activities) are those behaviors or specific activities you must do to achieve your expected end. Using the goal example above, activities might include:

- setting the alarm earlier
- choose the place and time for Bible study
- not planning anything else for that time frame
- turning phones and TVs off

You can be as creative as you want to be.

On the following pages, write down goals that you want to incorporate in your life and the subgoals or activities needed to achieve them, using the SMARTER way of setting goals.

LIFE DOMAIN GOALS

Life Domains (adjust the following to your needs)

SPIRITUAL GOALS: **Activities**

HEALTH AND FITNESS: **Activities**

JOB: **Activities**

EDUCATION: **Activities**

SOCIAL/FAMILY: **Activities**

RECREATION: **Activities**

FINANCIAL: Activities

List an area of your life and write down where you see God leading you in that area within the next year, 5 years, and 10 years. You can repeat this in any area of your life. If you do not have any direction right now, seek the Lord and begin to make plans but be ever watchful in case you are going off His path for you. He will let you know and guide you as you move out. Proverbs 16:9 states, "A man's heart plans his way, but the Lord directs his steps."

Proverb 16:3 promises, that when you "commit your works to the Lord, your thoughts will be established." How wonderful to know that He will give you clear and solid thoughts as you trust and obey Him!

Area:

1 year:

5 years:

10 years:

BIBLIOGRAPHY

Andrews, Andy. (2002). The Traveler's Gift. Tennessee: Thomas Nelson, Inc.

Beattie, Melody. (1987). Codependent No More. New York: Harper & Row.

Bender, Stephanie & Keleher, Kathleen. (1991). PMS—A Positive Program to Gain Control. New York: The Body Press.

Bennett, Dennis & Rita. (1971). The Holy Spirit and You. New Jersey: Logos International.

Berkhof, Louis. (1933). Manual of Christian Doctrine. Michigan: William B. Eerdmans Publishing Company.

Bradshaw, John. (1988). The Family. Florida: Health Communications, Inc.

Bridges, Jerry. (1978). The Pursuit of Holiness. Colorado: Navpress.

Bridges, Jerry. (1983). The Practice of Godliness. Colorado: Navpress.

Buhler, Rich. (1988). Pain and Pretending. Tennessee: Thomas Nelson, Inc.

Burkett, Larry. (1990). The Financial Planning Workbook. Chicago: Moody Press.

Campbell, Roderick. (1954). Israel and the New Covenant. Pennsylvania: Presbyterian and Reformed Publishing Company.

Cloud, H., & Townsend, J. (1992). Boundaries. Michigan: Zondervan Publishing House.

Corey, Gerald F. (1977). Theory and Practice of Counseling and Psychotherapy (2nd ed.). California: Wadsworth.

Dileo, Sandy. (1984). "Stress Management". California: Author.

Edman, V. Raymond. (1948). The Disciplines of Life. Minnesota: World Wide Publication.

Elwell, Walter A. (Editor). (1989). Evangelical Commentary on the Bible. Michigan: Baker Book House.

Engstrom, Ted W. (1976). The Making of a Christian Leader. Michigan: Zondervan Publishing House.

Erickson, Millard J. (1985). Christian Theology. Michigan: Baker Book House.

Esses, Michael. (1974). The Phenomenon of Obedience. New Jersey: Logos International.

Felber, Terry. (2002), Am I Making Myself Clear? Nashville: Thomas Nelson.

Foster, Richard. (1992). Prayer—Finding the Heart's True Home. California: Harper.

Fromm, Erich. (1956). The Art of Loving. New York: Harper & Row.

Green, Michael. (1975). I Believe in the Holy Spirit. Michigan: Wm. B. Eerdmans Publishing Company.

Hammond, Frank & Ida. (1973). Pigs In The Parlor. Missouri: Impact Books.

Hart, S.L. (1968). Lifetime of Love. Mass: Daughters of St. Paul.

Johnson, Spencer, MD. (1998). Who Moved My Cheese? USA: Penguin Group.

Lancaster, Wade & Jeanette. (1982). "Rational Decision Making: Managing Uncertainty". Journal of Nursing Administration. Sept. 1982. pgs. 23-28.

Leman, Dr. Kevin. (1981). Sex Begins in the Kitchen. California: Regal Books.

MacNutt, Francis, O.P. (1974). Healing. Indiana: Ave Maria Press.

Martin, Dr. Walter. (1962). Essential Christianity. California: GL Publications.

Martin, Francis P. (1979). Hung by the Tongue. Louisiana: F.P.M. Publications.

Maxwell, John C. (2023). The 16 Undeniable Laws of Communication. Maxwell Leadership Publishing

McAll, Dr. Kenneth. (1982). Healing the Family Tree. Great Britain: Sheldon Press.

Moody, Dwight L. (1881). Secret Power. California: Regal Books.

Murphy, Dr. Ed. (1992). The Handbook for Spiritual Warfare. Tennessee: Thomas Nelson Publishers, Inc.

Nutrition Search, Inc. (1973). Nutrition Almanac. New York: McGraw-Hill Book Company.

Payne, Leanne. (1991). Restoring the Christian Soul Through Healing Prayer. Illinois: Crossway Books.

Peck, M. Scott, MD. (1978). The Road Less Traveled. New York: Simon & Schuster, Inc.

Peck, M. Scott, MD. (1983). People of the Lie. New York: Simon & Schuster, Inc.

Penner, Clifford & Joyce. (1981). The Gift of Sex. Texas: Word, Inc.

Powell, John. (1969). Why Am I Afraid to Tell You Who I Am?. Illinois: Argus Communications.

Powell, John. (1974). The Secret of Staying in Love. Texas: Argus Communications.

Powell, John. (1976). Fully Human, Fully Alive. Illinois: Argus Communications.

Powell, John. (1978). Unconditional Love. Texas: Argus Communications.

Ross, Elisabeth Kübler-. (1960). On Death & Dying. Simon & Schuster/Touchstone.

Sanders, J. Oswald. (1967). Spiritual Leadership. Illinois: Moody Bible Institute.

Schaeffer, Francis A. (1971). True Spirituality. Illinois: Tyndale House Publishers.

Seamands, David A. (1981). Healing for Damaged Emotions. Illinois: SP Publications, Inc.

Smalley, Gary & Trent, John, Ph.D. (1986). The Blessing. Tennessee: Thomas Nelson, Inc.

Smalley, Gary & Trent, John, Ph.D. (1988). The Language of Love. California: Focus on the Family.

Smalley, Gary & Trent, John, Ph.D. (1990). The Two Sides of Love. Colorado: Focus on the Family.

Smith, Chuck. (1980). Effective Prayer Life. California: The Word for Today.

Swindoll, Charles R. (1983). Dropping Your Guard. New York: Bantam Books.

Taylor, Richard Shelley. (1962). The Disciplined Life. Minnesota: Bethany House Publishers.

Torrey, R.A. (1974 revised edition). The Person & Work of the Holy Spirit. Michigan: Zondervan Publishing House.

Vine, W. E. (1981). Vine's Expository Dictionary of Old and New Testament Words. New Jersey: Fleming H. Revell Company.

Watson, David. (1980). The Hidden Battle. Illinois: Harold Shaw Publishers.

White, Tom. (1993). Breaking Strongholds: How Spiritual Warfare Sets Captives Free. Michigan: Servant Publications.

Whitfield, Charles L., M.D. (1987). Healing the Child Within. Florida: Health Communications, Inc.

Wilkerson, David & Sherrill, John & Elizabeth. (1963). The Cross and The Switchblade. New Jersey: Spire Books.

Wilkerson, David. (1972). The Pocket Promise Book. California: Regal Books.

Williams, Dr. Roger J. (1971). Nutrition Against Disease. New York: Pitman Publishing Corporation.

ABOUT THE AUTHOR

My heart's cry is one of freedom and abundance for you, who read this. I was born and raised in the Panama Canal Zone and accepted Jesus Christ as my Lord and Savior between the ages of 10-13. During my childhood, God called me off by myself to spend time with Him reading His Word, next to the sparkling blue Caribbean water. He was my teacher and even with that, many mistakes did I make! When I was 17, He called me to be a Registered Nurse and it was during one of my areas of work that an earlier edition of this book was born.

I married at 22 to an unbeliever, was divorced at 30, and went through what I call baptism by fire during my first marriage. God had me clean up all I was doing that was unloving nor supporting my marriage regardless of what my ex-husband was or was not doing. Doing what is right because it is right, is the right thing to do though it's not easy. Especially when my own needs were not being met! An earlier edition of this book was completed during this season of life and I began teaching these kingdom principles of living a victorious life in the community for many years.

During the writing process, there were times that I stopped as I did not know what the next step was. I sought the Lord and He answered me through a sense of knowing. Only then did I move on and continued this journey. One summer, I remember sitting at my desk while the sun was shining brightly on the deep-colored greenery outside my window. I looked at everyone playing while I sat working with the sun playing on the leaves. I chose to not get up and play because, above all else, my heart's cry is one of freedom and abundance for you who read this. Even then, I knew that to create something requires sacrifice and I knew that I would either get my reward later or maybe never. And the reward didn't even matter. What was and still is important, is that I finish the work I promised God I would and was called to do.

I have since remarried, have a wonderful family, and look forward to more of God's blessings in my life as I give to others! May you ask Him for your way and follow it. Therein is fulfillment and blessings galore. Why else are we to be here but to live out what was ordained for each of us from the beginning of time? That is why this work was written. That is why this work was written for you.

With blessings always,
Nancy Williams

www.ingramcontent.com/pod-product-compliance
Lightning Source LLC
Chambersburg PA
CBHW060356050426
42449CB00009B/1762